The Ultimate Fashion Icon

T0364062

RP Minis®
Hachette Book Group
1290 Avenue of the Americas, New York, NY 10104
www.runningpress.com
@Running_Press

First Edition: October 2024

Published by RP Minis, an imprint of Hachette Book Group, Inc.
The RP Minis name and logo is a registered trademark of Hachette Book Group, Inc.

Running Press books may be purchased in bulk for business, educational, or promotional use. For more information, please contact your local bookseller or the Hachette Book Group Special Markets Department at Special.Markets@hbgusa.com.

The publisher is not responsible for websites (or their content) that are not owned by the publisher.

Design by Justine Kelley

ISBN: 978-0-7624-8792-9

Contents

A Fashion Icon for the Ages

No one in pop culture history has ever had a closet quite like Barbie. A peek inside her wardrobe reveals everything from ruffled ball gowns to space suits to retro swimsuits and Rollerblades, and the most famous designers in the world have been begging to dress her for decades. Since her debut in 1959, Barbie has been *the* ultimate fashion inspiration for generations, whether she's riding the range in cowgirl fringe and boots, leading a classroom as Teacher Barbie, or dressing to the nines for a Dream Date with Ken. She can be—and wear—it all.

Take a minute and think of your favorite Barbie outfit. (It's OK if you have more than one; after all, Barbie has *many* iconic looks.) Maybe it's the Barbie doll's first-ever ensemble, the classic black-and-white striped swimsuit paired with peep-toe mules, sunglasses, and a perky ponytail—an outfit that changed the toy landscape forever. Perhaps you're a fan of the iconic Peaches 'n Cream dress from the '80s, a sweet confection of billowing peach chiffon complete with a luxurious matching stole, or the Pucci-inspired minidress on the '90s bestseller Totally Hair Barbie. Or maybe your favorite Barbie outfit is one you styled on your own, mixing and matching pieces from her closet into a custom creation.

There's a reason Margot Robbie paid homage to so many of the Barbie doll's best looks on the red carpet while promoting the *Barbie* movie, including Schiaparelli's version of the strapless black Solo in the Spotlight

gown; a hot-pink mesh ode to Earring Magic Barbie; and a clever nod to 1985's working girl Day-to-Night Barbie, transforming from a classy business suit (complete with a matching hat, no less!) to a cocktail dress. These outfits are precious to Barbie fans and a testament to her incredible impact in the fashion world. Each one feels as fresh and timeless today as it did when it was introduced.

The Story Behind the Fashion

Much of the Barbie doll's covetable closet was designed by Carol Spencer, who worked at Mattel from 1963 to 1999 and played a huge role in shaping the Barbie doll's fashion-forward look. Clothing was always central to the Barbie doll's aesthetic; after all, she was created as a much more glamorous, older alternative to baby dolls, giving children the chance to act out their future fantasies and dreams. Barbie was an independent, unstoppable career woman who was doing life her way and dressing the part, and it was exciting to see yourself in her shoes no matter your age.

Spencer and her design team ensured that Barbie wasn't following the trends; she was setting them. Her wardrobe changed with the times, evolving from the dressy suits and separates of the early '60s to California-inspired denim in the '70s, lots of ruffles and sparkle in the opulent '80s, and the funkier silhouettes and styles of the '90s and beyond.

Barbie has also been dressed by some of the greatest fashion designers of all time, including Donna Karan, Dior, Versace, Bob Mackie, and Oscar de la Renta, among many others. She has slipped into Marilyn Monroe's white halter dress, David Bowie's baby-blue suit, Dorothy's magical ruby slippers, and everything in between. You name it, the Barbie doll has probably worn it. Today, there are more Barbie dolls than one could ever imagine—all with different hairstyles, body types, and personalities. The DreamHouse must have magical, ever-expanding closets to keep all these outfits in one place!

Spotlight on Your Style

Confused by your closet or ready to upgrade your signature style? Let these iconic Barbie dolls be your guide. Take the quiz and see which doll's fashion sense best aligns with yours and how to make yourself stand out in the crowd.

Q: How would you describe your personal style?

A: All glam, all the time

B: Colorful and trendy

C: Sporty

D: Ready for anything

Q: What's your favorite item in your closet?

A: A formal gown

B: A unique vintage piece no one else has

C: A bathing suit

D: A power suit

Q: It's Saturday afternoon. Where will we find you?

A: Getting ready with friends for a night out

B: At the thrift store looking for a unique piece

C: Relaxing at the beach

D: Practicing one of my many hobbies

Q: How do you like to unwind?

A: A luxe spa day

B: Shopping with friends

C: Getting outside

D: Reading or watching a
good TV series

Q: What do you love most about Barbie?

A: Her effortless glamour

B: Her innovative mindset

C: Her kindness

D: Her confidence

MOSTLY As:
SOLO IN THE SPOTLIGHT BARBIE

You're the ultimate icon and the epitome of class and sophistication. When people hear the word "glamour," they think of you. Lean into it with vintage-inspired dresses in classic shades of black and white. When in doubt, add a pop of red lipstick or a pair of high heels to turn up the glitz.

MOSTLY Bs:
TOTALLY HAIR BARBIE

No one does fashion quite like you. You love bright colors, bold prints, and true-to-you styles that feel fresh and fun. If it's trendy, you'll try it. Try sharing your style secrets with a friend, because fashion is more fun when you do it together!

MOSTLY Cs:
MALIBU BARBIE

You're all about enjoying the beauty of nature and soaking up the sun—responsibly, of course. (Don't forget your sunscreen!) Catch a wave in earth tones like sunset orange, '70s-style denim, flowy floral dresses, and a positive attitude.

MOSTLY Ds:

PRESIDENT BARBIE

We'd definitely trust you to lead the nation. You're confident, put together, and always on your game. You need outfits that can keep up with your busy lifestyle. Think suits and sheath dresses during the week and your favorite athleisure on the weekend; dressing the part should be fun!

You Can Be Anything!

But the secret to the Barbie doll's iconic style isn't a cute cocktail dress, great hair, and a shiny convertible to match. It's her confidence! Barbie knows that no matter what she's wearing, she's strong, smart, and worthy, and that's what makes her such an enduring icon for people of all ages, everywhere. There's a reason her motto is "You Can Be Anything!" Barbie knows that when you believe in yourself, anything is possible, and if a bright pink dress, structured suit, or even an astronaut helmet helps you take on the world, even better.

Need a little help connecting with your confidence and taking on the day? The secret may be hiding right in your closet, and there could be magic in that cozy sweater or LBD. When you're feeling more like dark gray than hot pink and want a sparkly boost in your life (and your closet!), channel Barbie! Take her penchant for bright colors, fashion-forward silhouettes, and well-placed plastic accessories and mix it up with what makes you feel good. Clothes have the power to change our mood in an instant; there's nothing like a perfectly fitted power suit for a big meeting, a colorful cocktail dress for girls' night, or a pair of worn-in sweatpants on the weekend.

As Barbie can attest, style is about trying new things, having fun, and wearing what makes you feel like the best version of you, no matter what others may think. With the right outfit and a big smile to match, the world is yours.

★ 32 ★